FLOWER POWER

Judith Heneghan and Diego Moscato

D1323228

Published in paperback in Great Britain in 2018 by Wayland

Editor: Nicola Edwards
Designer Anthony Hannant, Little Red Ant

ISBN: 978 1 5263 0764 4
Library eBook ISBN: 978 0 7502 8770 8

10 9 8 7 6 5 4 3 2 1

Wayland, an imprint of
Hachette Children's Group
Part of Hodder and Stoughton
Carmelite House
50 Victoria Embankment
London EC4Y 0DZ

An Hachette UK Company
www.hachette.co.uk
www.hachettechildrens.co.uk

Printed and bound in China

MIX
Paper from
responsible sources
FSC
www.fsc.org
FSC® C104740

2

Contents

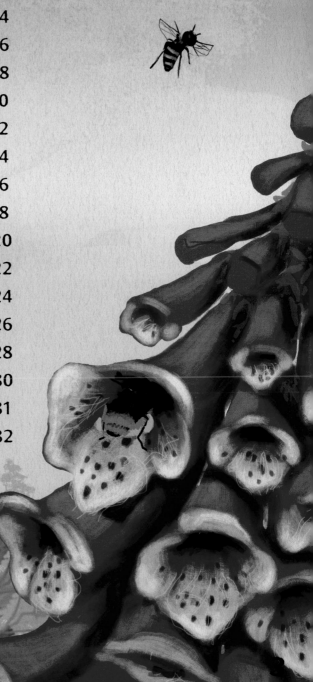

All around the world, plants grow in amazing variety. But why do flowers produce so many colours, shapes and scents? Read on to discover the wonderful ways in which flowers spread their pollen and so make new seeds.

On a sunny summer's morning, a flower bud bursts open. Silky red petals unfurl. The petals spread wide to face the warm sunshine. A hoverfly visits before buzzing away.

This is a field poppy. Its bright flower lasts for a single day.

The poppy's petals are brightly coloured to attract insects such as bees and hoverflies. Many plants need insects to help them make seeds and reproduce.

5

This bee is collecting pollen from a buttercup. Bees love to eat pollen, so they fly from flower to flower, gathering as much as they can. Tiny grains powder their bodies.

In this way, the bee carries pollen from one flower to another.

petal

stamen

carpel

Pollen sits on the tips of the stamens. Stamens
are the male part of the flower. The pollen needs
to reach the carpel which is the female part of the
flower. When pollen reaches the sticky surface of
the carpel, the flower is pollinated.

Animals that spread pollen are called pollinators.

7

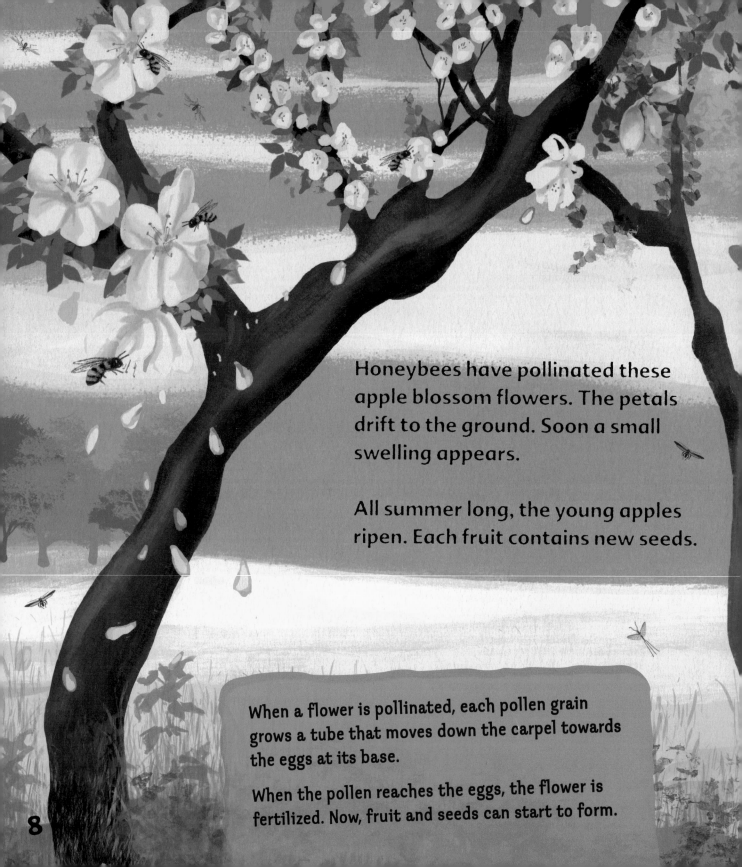

Honeybees have pollinated these apple blossom flowers. The petals drift to the ground. Soon a small swelling appears.

All summer long, the young apples ripen. Each fruit contains new seeds.

When a flower is pollinated, each pollen grain grows a tube that moves down the carpel towards the eggs at its base.

When the pollen reaches the eggs, the flower is fertilized. Now, fruit and seeds can start to form.

When this willow-herb flower first opens, the stamens stretch out. They are loaded with pollen for insects to take away.

The carpel waits until the stamens have withered. Now it pushes forwards, sticky and ripe, ready for pollen from another willow-herb plant.

Flowers can only be fertilized with pollen
from the same species. The healthiest seeds
form when the pollen comes from another
plant of the same species. So many flowers
keep their male and female parts separate.
This stops them pollinating themselves.

A tortoiseshell butterfly settles on a knapweed plant, but it isn't searching for pollen. This butterfly wants the nectar stored inside each flower. While its long tongue sucks up the sugary liquid, some pollen grains stick to its legs.

Many flowers produce nectar to attract insects and birds. They depend on the energy it supplies.

Look closely and you'll see that the knapweed flower is really lots of flowers, each with its own stamens, carpel and nectar supply.

These garden flowers show off their colours. Bright petals signal a sweet nectar treat. Red, yellow, purple, orange — insects soon fly in to feast.

Some flowers use several colours to create a target for pollinators. If an insect reaches the target, it will find the nectar.

Insects are attracted to colours. However, they don't 'see' colour the same way we do. Different coloured flowers are preferred by different insects.

Flowers use shape as well as colour to attract the pollinators they need. This foxglove has a long spike of flowers that reaches high into the air. The petals of each flower are joined to make a tunnel. The tunnel has a lip to land on, and spots act like markers to show the way inside.

Foxgloves need a large bee to pick up their pollen. So the lip of each flower is covered with tiny hairs that make it difficult for smaller insects to land.

These flat ox-eye daisies aren't so particular. Their open shape provides an easy landing for most insects.

17

This hummingbird hovers by a trumpet vine. Its beak and head fit perfectly into the long, slender flower.

Pollen grains stick to the hummingbird when it pushes deep inside the flower to drink the nectar.

The same is true for this long-nosed bat, feeding on a cactus flower at night.

19

Some plants don't flower in the day. Their petals open as darkness falls. So night-time pollinators like moths rely on smell rather than colour to find them. A sphinx moth seeks out these evening primrose flowers by following their special scent.

Flowers that are pollinated in the dark don't need bright colours. They rely on strong scent, and often have pale flowers that show up in the moonlight.

This corpse flower smells like its name: it stinks of decaying meat. This rotten stench attracts blow flies and beetles that feed on the flesh of dead animals. But the smell is just a clever trick to tempt the insects inside.

There are several different kinds of corpse flower, most growing in south-east Asia. All are coloured red, brown and purple — just like rotting meat.

This bright red corpse flower holds several litres of nectar!

The mirror orchid is shaped like a female wasp. It smells like a female wasp. And its shiny blue surface copies the reflection of the sky on a female wasp's wings.

A male wasp soon lands, hoping to find a mate. He's going to be disappointed! The only prize here is a few grains of pollen.

There are lots of different orchid plants and many have adapted in unique ways to trick insects into visiting them.

25

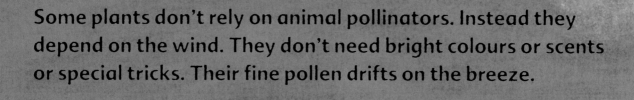

Some plants don't rely on animal pollinators. Instead they depend on the wind. They don't need bright colours or scents or special tricks. Their fine pollen drifts on the breeze.

Grasses and trees are often pollinated by the wind. Their flowers are small and pale and they produce large amounts of pollen to increase the chance of it reaching other plants.

This ragweed plant releases up to a billion grains of pollen in a year. Its pollen is so light it can remain in the air for several days and may travel hundreds of kilometres.

Flowers are the stars of the pollination story, though insects, birds, mammals and the wind all play their part.

Flowers give us fruit, nuts, grain and seed for new plants. They amaze us in all their variety.

This passion fruit flower is beautiful to look at with its bright target colours. It has a sweet fragrance and provides lots of nectar for its main pollinators — birds and bees. It also produces delicious fruit, packed with seeds.

Things to do

Grow your own meadow flowers! It takes three to four months to grow them from seed. In the middle of spring, scatter seeds such as field poppies, cornflowers, corn marigold and corncockles over a patch of waste ground or bare earth, or plant them in a tub. Make sure the soil has good natural daylight and keep it moist, but not too wet.

You should see green shoots appearing after two to three weeks, with flowers blooming about three months later. Watch for any visiting pollinators!

Glossary

carpel — the female part of the flower

fertilised — when pollen reaches an egg at the base of the carpel

nectar — the sweet liquid produced by flowers; food for many insects
and birds

petals — the outside parts of the flower

pollen — tiny grains that form at the tips of the stamens

pollinated — when pollen lands on the carpel, which is the female part of
the flower

pollinator — an animal that carries pollen from one flower to another

species — a specific type of plant or animal

stamen — the male part of the flower

Further information

- Did you know that scientists have counted around 400,000 different species of flowering plants in the world? More species are being discovered all the time.

- Honeybees may visit up to 2,000 flowers in a day.

- Flower petals are used to make perfume, dye for cloth, and even some medicines.

- The tallest sunflower ever grown was over eight and a half metres — that's the height of four men!

Index